In This Bedroom

Nancy Harris

Raintree

Chicago, Illinois

www.heinemannraintree.com

Visit our website to find out more information about Heinemann-Raintree books.

To order:

☎ Phone 888-454-2279

💻 Visit www.heinemannraintree.com to browse our catalog and order online.

2010 Raintree Library
an imprint of Capstone Global Library, LLC
Chicago, Illinois

Edited by Rebecca Rissman, Nancy Dickmann, and Sian Smith
Designed by Joanna Hinton-Malivoire
Original illustrations © Capstone Global Library LLC, 2010
Illustrated by Kevin Rechin
Picture research by Tracy Cummins
Originated by Capstone Global Library Ltd
Printed and bound in China by Leo Paper Products Ltd

14 13 12 11 10
10 9 8 7 6 5 4 3 2 1

Library of Congress Cataloging-in-Publication Data
Harris, Nancy, 1956-
  In this bedroom / Nancy Harris.
    p. cm. -- (What's lurking in this house?)
  Includes bibliographical references and index.
  ISBN 978-1-4109-3723-0 (hc)
  ISBN 978-1-4109-3729-2 (pb) 1. Household pests--Juvenile literature. 2. Bedrooms--Juvenile literature. 3. House cleaning--Juvenile literature. I. Title.
  TX325.H274 2010
  648'.7--dc22
                    2009022149

Acknowledgments
The author and publisher are grateful to the following for permission to reproduce copyright material: Alamy pp.**16**, **18** (© Nigel Cattlin), **27** (© Nikki Edmunds); Bugwood.org p.**17** (© Clemson University - USDA Cooperative Extension Slide Series); Getty Images pp.**7** bottom (Nigel Cattlin), **10** (Dag Sundberg), **15** (John Downer); Photo Researchers, Inc. pp.**7 center** (© Andrew Syred), **9** (© Eye of Science), **12** (© Andrew Syred), **21** (©Kenneth Eward), **23** (© David M. Phillips), **25** (© Julie Dermansky); Photolibrary p.**26** (Marc Gilsdorf); Shutterstock pp. **7 top** (© 6493866629), **8** (© Oberon), **13** (© Chris Rodenberg Photography), **20** (© Evok20), **29 bedbug** (© Artur Tiutenko), **29 mold** (© Robert Adrian Hillman), **29 office** (© terekhov igor); SuperStock p.**28** (Brand X).

Cover photograph of bedbugs reproduced with permission of Science Photo Library (Eye of Science).

Every effort has been made to contact copyright holders of any material reproduced in this book. Any omissions will be rectified in subsequent printings if notice is given to the publisher.

All the Internet addresses (URLs) given in this book were valid at the time of going to press. However, due to the dynamic nature of the Internet, some addresses may have changed, or sites may have changed or ceased to exist since publication. While the author and publisher regret any inconvenience this may cause readers, no responsibility for any such changes can be accepted by either the author or the publisher.

Some words are shown in bold, **like this**. You can find out what they mean by looking in the glossary.

Contents

Is Something Lurking in This House?

A house is a place where you eat, sleep, work, and play. You sleep and sometimes work or play in the bedroom. But do you ever think about what may be living in your bedroom?

Bedtime

It's bedtime. You lie down on your bed, rest your head on the pillow, and pull up the covers. You turn off the light. It is just you and your bed in the dark. Or is it? What else is lurking in your bedroom?

Tiny Crawlers

As you sleep, very tiny bugs called dust mites move around your bedroom. They are so small you need to use a **microscope** to see them.

Dust mites often live in mattresses and carpets.

microscope

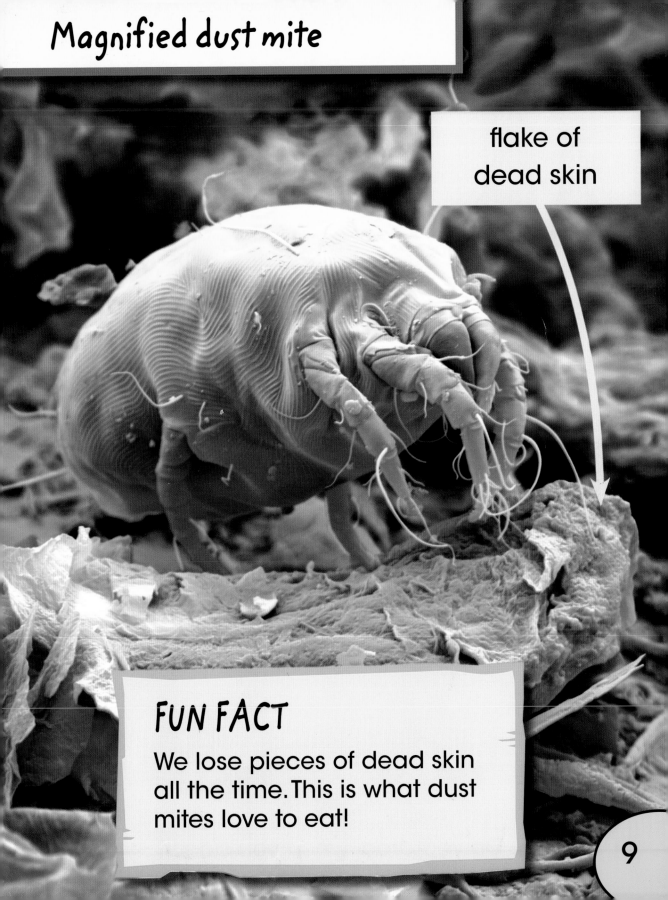

Magnified dust mite

flake of
dead skin

FUN FACT

We lose pieces of dead skin
all the time. This is what dust
mites love to eat!

10

Do you drool when you sleep?

Dust mites like to live in warm places. They also like to be near wet or **moist** places. This is why they live in your mattress and pillow. Your body's heat and sweat keeps them warm and damp. So does your drool.

Blood-Sucking Bedbugs

Some unlucky people have bedbugs living in their bedrooms. You don't need a **microscope** to spot bedbugs. They are about the size of an apple seed.

bedbug

Bedbugs can hide in your bed or even on stuffed toys.

Bedbugs usually come out and eat at night. They are **parasites**. This means they live off of other animals. They bite people as they sleep and drink their blood.

bedbug

15

Tasty Sweaters

Have you ever spotted a hole in one of your sweaters? It could have been eaten by a young clothes moth. Young clothes moths are called **larvae**. They are white and look like worms.

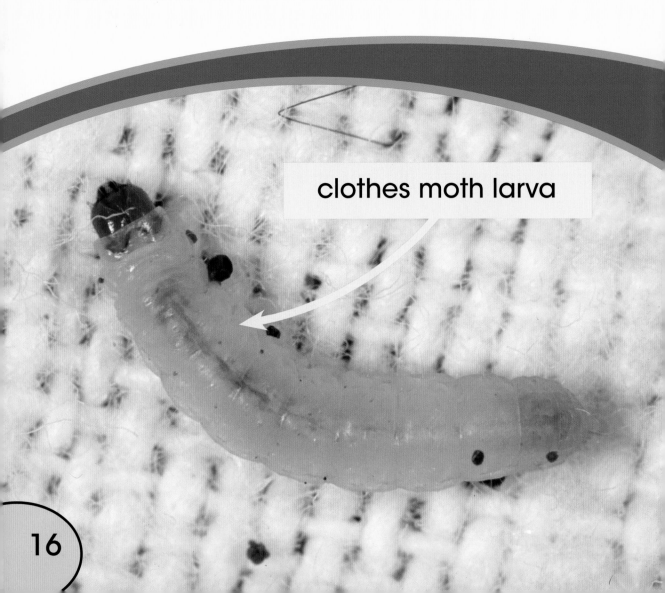

clothes moth larva

Adult clothes moths can be white, gray, or brown in color. They can be ½ inch long. That is about the same length as a sunflower seed.

adult clothes moth

17

case

Some larvae make feeding cases
to hide in. They can stay in these
while they eat the clothes.

Clothes moths **larvae**, or young, like to eat wool, hair, and feathers. They like to eat in dark and quiet places. Your bedroom closet is a great place for these insects to eat. It is dark and full of tasty things for them to munch on.

Germ Busting

Many other things live in your bedroom. **Germs** are another thing to watch out for. Germs are very small living things that can cause illness. You need to use a **microscope** to see germs.

FUN FACT

One of the main places you can find germs is on your mattress and bedding. Change your sheets often!

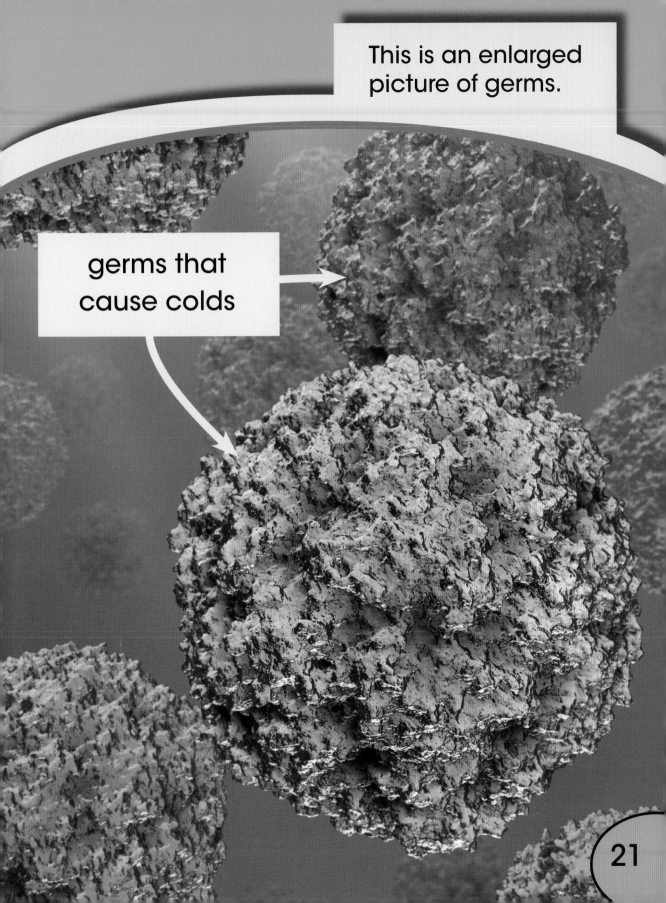

Hungry Bacteria

Bacteria are a type of **germ**. You can only see bacteria under a **microscope**. Bacteria can be found almost anywhere. They are on your pillow, mattress, and clothing. Some bacteria can make you sick.

FUN FACT

Bacteria can even be found on your alarm clock button!

Bacteria are not picky eaters. They eat the dead skin that can be found all over a bedroom.

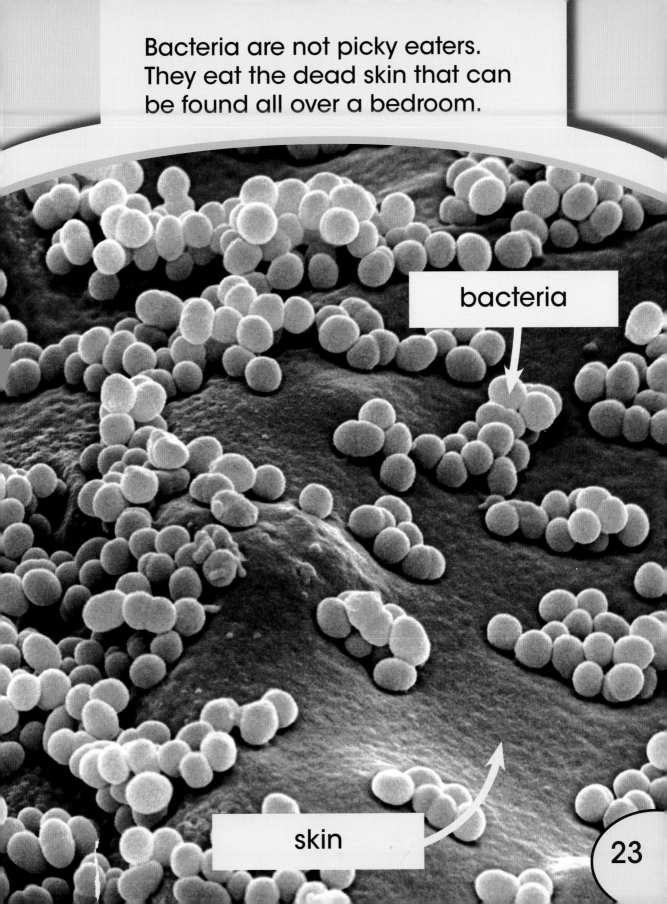

bacteria

skin

Growing in the Corner

Mold is a small living thing. Mold likes to live in warm places. Mold can only live in wet or **moist** places. Your bedroom can be moist and warm.

mold

mold

Mold can make you sick. Look out for mold in your bedroom!

You could see blue mold on your carpet. You could see white mold on your wallpaper. You could see black mold on your ceiling.

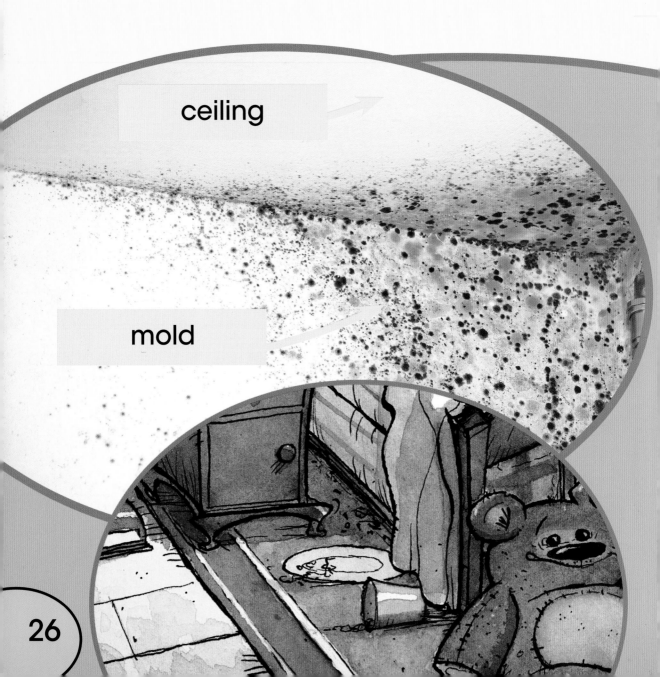

ceiling

mold

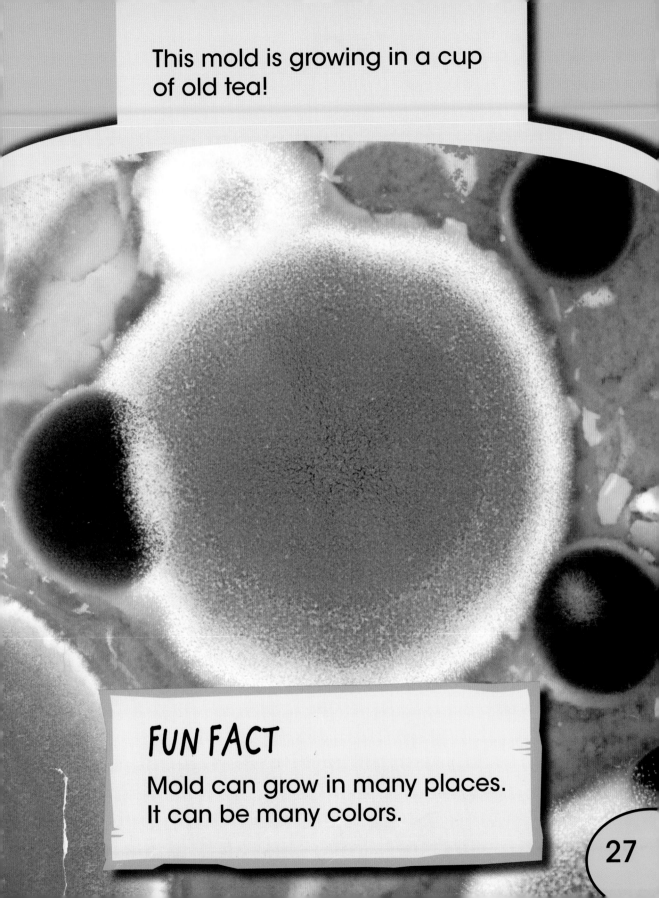

This mold is growing in a cup of old tea!

FUN FACT

Mold can grow in many places. It can be many colors.

Keeping It Clean

You never know what might be lurking in your bedroom. Vacuum your carpets and floor. Wash your clothes and sheets. This will help to reduce the amount of creatures and **germs** in your bedroom.

Fun Facts

The average desk has more than 10,000 germs living on it.

Bedbugs die at high temperatures. Putting bedding in a tumble dryer kills them off.

Bedbugs have a flat shape. This helps them to hide in narrow spaces.

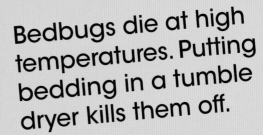

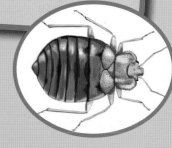

There are about 150 different types of house mold.

Approximately three dust mites can fit into the period at the end of this sentence.

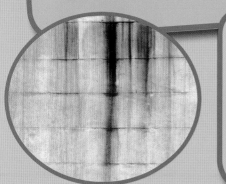

Glossary

bacteria tiny living things. Bacteria are a type of germ.

germs tiny living things that can make you ill if they get inside your body

larvae the young of some types of insect

microscope instrument used to see very small things such as germs

moist wet or damp

parasites living things that feed off of other living things

Find Out More

Books

Lockwood, Sophie. *Moths.* Mankato, MN: Child's World 2008.

Oetting, Judy. *Germs.* Danbury, CT: Children's Press, 2006.

Ridley, Sarah. *Where to Find Minibeasts: Minibeasts in the Home.* Mankato, MN: Smart Apple Media, 2009.

Sexton, Colleen. *Beetles.* Minneapolis: Bellweather Media, 2007.

Taylor-Butler, Christine. *Tiny Life on Your Body.* Danbury, CT: Children's Press, 2005.

Websites

http://kidshealth.org/kid/talk/qa/germs.html
This section on the Kid's Health Website tells you about germs and how to protect yourself from them.

http://pestworldforkids.org/bedbugs.html
This Website tells you about bedbugs. It includes information on what they eat, where they live and how to keep them out of your house.

Index